LIVI

The Middle Ages

Written by Bart Tesoriero
Illustrations by Michael Adams

TABLE OF CONTENTS

Library of Congress Control Number: 2012905935
ISBN 1-617960-50-5

SAINT ANTHONY

Feast Day: June 13

Patron of Lost Things and Missing Persons

Saint Anthony was born in Portugal in 1195 and became a Franciscan at the age of 26. God gave him the gift of preaching to touch the hearts of his listeners. When Saint Anthony spoke about Jesus and his Mother Mary, many people returned to Jesus and the Catholic faith. Saint Anthony asked Mary to help him when he preached, and God worked many miracles through him. One night, a friend saw a beautiful little Child standing upon a book, and clinging with both of His little arms around Anthony's neck. It was the Infant Jesus! Saint Anthony died at the age of 36, and the very next year he was canonized a saint.

Prayer to Saint Anthony to Find Lost Articles

Dear Saint Anthony, God has made you a powerful patron and helper to find lost or misplaced objects. We turn to you today with confidence and love. Through your prayer, may God help us to find what we have lost. Dear Saint Anthony, help us also be close to Jesus this day, and to always find Him in our hearts. Amen.

Saint Anthony, pray for us.

THOMAS · AQUINAS

SAINT THOMAS AQUINAS

Feast Day: January 28
Patron of Students

Saint Thomas Aquinas was born into a noble Italian family around 1226. When he was 17, he joined the Dominican Order, against his family's wishes. His brothers kidnapped him and held him prisoner for two years in their castle. However, Thomas escaped and went to Germany to study under Saint Albert the Great. He became a priest and was sent to the University of Paris, where he taught philosophy and theology for many years.

Saint Thomas deeply loved Our Lord Jesus. He wrote special prayers and hymns about the Blessed Sacrament. He wrote many books to help Christians understand more about Jesus and our faith. Saint Thomas Aquinas died in 1274. He was named one of the 33 Doctors, or Teachers, of the Church.

Prayer to Saint Thomas Aquinas for Students

Dear Saint Thomas Aquinas, please pray for all students. Help them to study well about God and all He has created. Help them to love wisdom and truth. Through your prayers, may God's light shine on us all. Amen.

Saint Thomas Aquinas, pray for us!

SAINT PEREGRINE
Feast Day: May 4
Patron of Cancer Patients

Saint Peregrine was born in 1260 in Italy. He enjoyed many fine pleasures and riches. At the age of 30, he accepted Jesus as his Lord, was baptized, and gave his life to God. Saint Peregrine became a priest in an order of men called the Servants of Mary, or the Servites. He spent his life caring for the sick, the poor, and the forgotten. At the age of 60, he was diagnosed with a severe cancer in his leg.

The night before his leg was to be amputated, Peregrine dragged himself before the crucifix and begged Jesus to heal him. In a vision, he saw Jesus lean down from the Cross to touch and heal his leg. Saint Peregrine died on May 1, 1345 and was canonized on December 27, 1726.

Prayer to Saint Peregrine for Cancer Patients

O great Saint Peregrine, in a vision you saw Jesus coming down from His Cross to heal you. Please ask God to bless and heal all those who suffer from cancer and skin disease. May He also bless their families and those who care for them. In Jesus' name. Amen.

Saint Peregrine, pray for us.

SAINT ROCH

Feast Day: August 16

Patron of All who Heal Contagious Diseases

Saint Roch was born with a red cross on his chest in the year 1295 in France. His parents died when he was a young man, and he joined the Third Order of Saint Francis. Roch cared for victims of the plague, a serious disease, in Rome. He healed many people by making the sign of the Cross over them. Then one day, Roch also became sick. He went into the forest to die, but a dog became his friend. The dog took food from his master's table, and brought it to Roch. In time, Roch got better!

Roch returned to town but was put into prison by mistake. An angel cared for him there until his death five years later. The day Roch died, his father came into his cell and recognized him by the cross on his chest. Saint Roch, or Rocco, was canonized 100 years after his death.

Prayer to Saint Roch for All who Heal Diseases

Dear Saint Roch, God's power in you was so great that many people were healed of their diseases. Please join us in asking Our Lord Jesus to heal all who suffer from disease and to bless those who serve them. Amen.

Saint Roch, pray for us.

SAINT CATHERINE OF SIENA

Feast Day: April 29

Patron of Nurses

Saint Catherine of Siena was born on March 25, 1347, in Siena, Italy. As a young girl, she had visions of angels. At the age of 15, Catherine entered the Third Order of Saint Dominic. She loved to pray quietly alone with God, and then serve others with love and joy. Catherine traveled through Italy, bringing people back to obedience to the Pope, and winning hardened souls to God.

Saint Catherine died at the age of 33. In 1970, Pope Paul VI declared Saint Catherine of Siena and Saint Teresa of Avila to be the first women Doctors, or Teachers, of the Church.

Prayer to Saint Catherine of Siena for Nurses

Dear Saint Catherine, because of your devotion to Jesus, God used you to bring healing to the world. Lord God, through the prayers of Saint Catherine of Siena, please bless all nurses. Heal every person who is in their care. May their loving attention and kindness help draw their patients to You. In Jesus' name we pray. Amen.

Saint Catherine of Siena, pray for us!

SAINT VINCENT FERRER

Feast Day: April 5

Patron of Plumbers

Saint Vincent Ferrer was born on January 23, 1350, in Valencia, Spain. His father dreamed that Vincent would grow up to be a famous friar. At 18, Vincent joined the Dominicans. After much study, he became a master of sacred theology. He loved and memorized God's Word as well.

In 1398, Vincent became very sick from sadness, since the Church was divided by a Great Schism. Our Lord Jesus appeared to Vincent in a vision and healed him. He told Vincent to preach and tell everyone to repent and be holy. For the next 21 years, he preached and worked stupendous miracles throughout Europe, converting thousands of people.

Saint Vincent was so successful at building up the Church that today he is remembered as the patron of the building trades and of plumbers in particular. He died in 1419.

Prayer to Saint Vincent Ferrer for Plumbers

Dear Saint Vincent, by opening yourself up to God, you allowed His grace to flow into the lives of many. Dear God, through the prayers of Saint Vincent, bless all plumbers, and all who build up Your Church. In Jesus' name. Amen.

Saint Vincent Ferrer, pray for us.

SAINT BERNARDINE OF SIENA

Feast Day: May 20
Patron of Advertisers

Saint Bernardine was born in 1380 in Siena, Italy. He joined the Franciscans in 1402 and was ordained two years later. His voice was very weak because of an illness. Through the prayers of Our Mother Mary, he was healed and began preaching.

When preaching, Saint Bernardine would often hold up a card with the name of Jesus. He urged people to turn to Our Lord and accept His grace. Saint Bernardine preached for the rest of his life and died in 1444.

Saint Bernardine was canonized a saint in 1450. He is the patron of advertisers because he was very gifted at persuading people to love God and do good.

Prayer to Saint Bernardine of Siena for Advertisers

Saint Bernardine, through your preaching, thousands of people returned to God. Help all people who work as advertisers to be wise and good. Dear God, through the prayers of Saint Bernadine, please help advertisers to use their skills for Your glory and the good of others. Help all of us to be Your witnesses in all we do and say. In Jesus' name. Amen.

Saint Bernardine of Siena, pray for us.

SAINT RITA

Feast Day: May 22
Patron of Parents

Saint Rita was born in Italy in 1381. She wanted to become a nun, but her parents arranged for her to marry a man named Mancini. Rita obediently married him and gave birth to two sons. 18 years passed and Mancini was stabbed to death by an enemy. Rita prayed for him and he gave his soul to Jesus before he died. Her sons also died, and Rita became a nun. She lived 40 years in the convent, in great prayer and charity, working for peace in the area.

Rita loved Jesus very much. One day her forehead was miraculously pierced by a thorn from the Crown of Thorns. After suffering 15 years, Saint Rita died in 1457. Saint Rita loved her husband, her family, and her fellow sisters as a wife, a mother, a widow, and a nun.

Prayer to Saint Rita for Parents

Dear Saint Rita, please bless my Mom and Dad, and all parents. Help them to feel God's love in their hearts for one another and for us their children. Protect them through your prayers and help them to be happy together forever. Amen.

Saint Rita, pray for us.

SAINT JOAN OF ARC

Feast Day: May 30

Patron of Servicewomen

Saint Joan of Arc was born in France in 1412. One day, as she cared for the sheep on her family farm, she heard the voices of some of the saints. They told Joan to help the king of France fight his enemies.

At the young age of 17, Joan went to help the king. She won the battle for Orleans, France, with a small army. She won many more battles, and helped the king to regain the throne of France.

The king's enemies kidnapped Joan and put her in prison. Joan was condemned to death because she refused to lie and say the saints had not spoken to her. She was burned at the stake on May 30, 1431, at the age of 19. However, the Church later canonized her as Saint Joan of Arc.

Prayer to Saint Joan of Arc

Dear Saint Joan of Arc, God gave you great skill in fighting for France. Through your prayers may He bless all women who love and stand up for their families, their country, and their Faith. In Jesus' name. Amen

Saint Joan of Arc, pray for us.

SAINT THOMAS MORE

Feast Day: June 22
Patron of Lawyers

Saint Thomas More was born in London in 1478. He studied law at Oxford University and was elected to Parliament. In 1501, Thomas became a lawyer and began his career as a civil servant. King Henry VIII appointed him as Lord Chancellor of England in 1529. Saint Thomas refused to honor the King as the Head of the Church of England and was confined to the Tower of London, where he was convicted of treason. Saint Thomas More was beheaded on July 6, 1535. He told the crowd, "I die as the King's good servant—but God's first!" Because of his honesty and fairness, Saint Thomas is recognized today as the patron of attorneys and lawyers.

Prayer to Saint Thomas More for Attorneys

Dear Saint Thomas, you dedicated your life to learning the truth. You served your king, but you served God first. Dear God, through the intercession of Saint Thomas More, please bless all lawyers and attorneys. Give them the courage to stand up for truth and justice, even if they must stand alone. Let them know You will never leave them nor forsake them. In Jesus' name. Amen.

Saint Thomas More, pray for us.

SAINT JOHN OF GOD

Feast Day: March 8
Patron of Printers and Publishers

Saint John of God was born in 1495 in Portugal. He left home as a young boy, but soon fell ill and was abandoned. A shepherd found John and cared for him. Then John left to become a soldier. As a soldier he did many things he would later regret.

One day John heard Saint John of Avila preach a sermon. John became aware of his sins and realized he needed to repent and return to God. He started his own hospital for all the poor and sick. He died in 1550 after ten years of service and was canonized in 1690.

Prayer to Saint John of God for Printers and Publishers

Dear Saint John, when you realized your sins had hurt God and others, you repented of them. You changed your life and set a new path for yourself. Through your many loving deeds, you revealed God's compassion and drew countless people to Him. Dear God, through the prayers of Saint John, bless all who work in printing and publishing. Help them to share Your love with others and to help people live good lives. In Jesus' name we pray. Amen.

Saint John of God, pray for us.

SAINT IGNATIUS OF LOYOLA

Feast Day: July 31
Patron of Educators and Retreatants

Saint Ignatius was born at Loyola, Spain, in the year 1491. After being wounded in battle, he decided to serve Jesus as his King. Ignatius went to study at the University of Paris, where several young men joined him to serve Christ. They were known as the "Companions of Jesus," or the Jesuits. "The Companions," said Ignatius, "are ready to do any work or go anywhere in the world for God's greater glory." They became famous teachers, and continued to serve the poor, living and teaching as soldiers of Christ.

Saint Ignatius suffered many trials, but he trusted in God, and composed his famous "Spiritual Exercises." Saint Ignatius died on July 31, 1556.

Prayer to Saint Ignatius of Loyola for Educators

Dear Saint Ignatius, you loved helping others to find Jesus in their hearts and souls. You loved learning because as we learn more about God, we are able to love Him more. Please pray for all teachers to help their students find God's truth and also His love. Amen.

Saint Ignatius, pray for us.

SAINT FRANCIS XAVIER

Feast Day: December 3
Patron of Missionaries

Saint Francis Xavier was born to noble parents in Spain in 1506. He enjoyed sports and school. He attended the University of Paris where he met Saint Ignatius of Loyola. Ignatius helped Francis give himself to Jesus Christ. Francis and some companions helped Saint Ignatius establish the Society of Jesus—*the Jesuits*—and he was ordained a priest in 1537. He sailed to India and baptized thousands of people from there to Japan. Saint Francis set out for China, and died within sight of that great country in 1552. Saint Francis Xavier is considered the greatest missionary since Saint Paul. In 1904, Pope Saint Pius X proclaimed him the patron of all foreign missions.

Prayer to Saint Francis Xavier for Missionaries

Dear Saint Francis Xavier, God called you to preach the Gospel to the peoples of India and Asia. Please pray for all those who bring God's good news to people in far away lands. Dear God, through the prayers of Your servant Saint Francis Xavier, help us to feel Your love burning in our hearts. Help us to be not afraid to speak of You to all we meet. In Jesus' name. Amen.

Saint Francis Xavier, pray for us.

SAINT TERESA OF AVILA

Feast Day: October 15

Patron of People Suffering with Headaches

Saint Teresa was born in Avila, Spain in 1515. When Teresa was only 12 years old, her mother died and her father placed her in a convent. During this time Teresa suffered from painful headaches. She was cured through the prayers of Saint Joseph. Teresa realized that God was calling her to make her convent a holier place, so she reformed the Carmelites. She established 32 monasteries. She also wrote many letters and books which have helped people learn more about prayer and God's love for them.

Saint Teresa died in 1582, was canonized in 1622, and was named the first woman Doctor of the Church in 1970. Saint Teresa of Avila is recognized today as the patroness of those suffering with headaches or migraines.

Prayer to Saint Teresa of Avila for Headache Sufferers

Dear Saint Teresa, You followed Jesus Christ, who loved us so much that He chose to be crucified for us. Please pray for all who suffer from headaches, that God will heal them and grant them His peace. Amen.

Saint Teresa of Avila, pray for us.

SAINT CHARLES BORROMEO

Feast Day: November 4
Patron of Catechists and Seminarians

Saint Charles was born in 1538 to a noble family in Italy. He was ordained a priest in 1563 and was consecrated bishop of Milan the same year. By wise laws, by gentle kindness and by his own marvelous example, Saint Charles made his diocese a model for the whole Church. He faithfully prayed and did penance, gave everything he owned to the poor, and set up altars in the streets to bring Mass to the ill.

In 1571, the whole province of Milan suffered from a terrible famine and, later, a plague. Saint Charles worked very hard to help the starving and others who were sick due to the food shortage. He died in 1584.

Prayer to Saint Charles for Seminarians and Catechists

Dear Saint Charles Borromeo, you helped seminarians, priests, and other people to know God better. Please pray for all who teach us about Jesus and our Catholic Faith. Help them to share the love and goodness of Jesus with us, that we might love God and love one another. Amen.

Saint Charles Borromeo, pray for us.

THE MIDDLE AGES

The Middle Ages, from roughly 1,000 to 1500 AD, were an exciting but difficult time in Europe. They began with the Norman invasion of England and saw the rise of kingdoms in Europe and Asia, the struggle between Muslims and Crusaders, the Renaissance, and the discovery of the New World. The only recognized religion in Europe was Catholic Christianity, and the Church was a major influence, whether you were a peasant or a king.

The Church began many early universities, such as the University of Paris, where saints like Albert the Great and Thomas Aquinas taught the classics, philosophy, and theology. Meanwhile, orators like Saint Vincent Ferrer preached the Gospel fervently from Spain to Scotland.

Missionaries like Saint Francis Xavier left home and family to bring the Good News to far away places like India, Japan, and even China! Saint Joan of Arc helped drive the English from France, and reformers like Saint Teresa of Avila renewed the faith and spirituality of their orders.

Dear Saints of the Middle Ages, you delighted in God's love for you and you gave yourself completely to Him in return. Please help me, like you, to love God and to make this world a better place for His sake. Amen.